GET THE POINT

A Beginner's Guide to Essay Writing, Critical Thinking Skills & Logical Reasoning

– ARMANITALKS 🎙️🔥

Copyright © 2021 Arman N. Chowdhury

All rights reserved. This book or any portion thereof may not be reproduced or used in any manner whatsoever without the express written permission of the publisher except for the use of brief quotations in a book review.

Printed in the United States of America¬
First Printing, 2022

https://www.armanitalks.com

CONTENTS

Introduction 7

Part 1: Fundamentals 13

What to Expect 15
What is Logic? 17
What is Critical Thinking? 23
Understanding Words 27

Part 2: What are Essays? 33

What to Expect 35
Essay Writing 101 37
Popular Types of Essays 39
Difference Between Essays and Short Stories 45
Making a Point 49

Part 3: Research and Development 55

What to Expect 57
Know A Lot 59
Reputable Sources 63
Personal Experience 67

Part 4: Creating a Skeleton 71

What to Expect 73
Importance of Outlining your Essays 75
Formal Outlining Method 79
Informal Outlining Method 83

Part 5: How to Create 87

What to Expect 89
Creation Mindset 91
Rough Draft 95
Over Write 97

    Timer = Best Friend 99

Part 6: How to Edit 103

    What to Expect 105
    What is Editing? 107
    My Editing Process 109

Part 7: How to Proofread 115

    What to Expect 117
    1 - Do it Yourself 119
    2 - Hire Someone to Proofread 121

Part 8: PUBLISH! 123

    What to Expect 125
    Importance of Publishing 127
    Read Back your Old Content 129

Part 9: Creating an Empire with Essays ... 133

    What to Expect 135
    Practice Makes Progress 139
    Solidify your Writing Process 141
    Generational Ideas 143

Final Words 145

|Introduction

Don't you hate it when someone is talking for a long time, but you have no clue what they are saying?

Mentally, you may be waving your hand in a circular motion like:
'Alright buddy, get to the point already!'

Well, here's the thing…
Getting to the point is **earned**.

It's not a gift that is given to someone without work ethic, a solid writing practice, and daily refinement in critical thinking skills.

Get To The Point

This book will teach you the art and science of essay writing.

You may have a very negative perception of essay writing at this stage of your life.

Maybe in school, the teacher sucked the life out of writing essays with their excessive formulas and rigid ways of thinking.

'Use the thumb to make an indent!!' they said.

But if you understand the purpose of essays, then it becomes a pleasure to write them.

You no longer write essays because you have to.
You write essays because you want to.

Essays are a great way to:
- Clarify your thinking.
- Make your points.
- Persuade others.
- And dare I say...create yourself.

Introduction

Since this a beginner's guide to essay writing, we aren't going to be using any fancy terminologies or pompous language.

We are going to get straight to the point so you can start creating meaningful essays in:
- School
- Work
- Business

And much more!

The essay writing process discussed in this book is:
1. Create your context.
2. Research.
3. Create a skeleton.
4. Create a rough draft.
5. Edit.
6. Proofread.
7. Publish.

Before we get started, let me quickly introduce myself.

My name is Arman Chowdhury, the founder of ArmaniTalks.

Get To The Point

ArmaniTalks is a media company that helps engineers and entrepreneurs improve their communication skills so they can articulate their ideas with clarity and confidence.

The 6-core soft skills that the ArmaniTalks brand covers includes:
- Concentration
- Emotional intelligence
- Creativity
- Storytelling
- Public speaking
- Social skills

The brand shares its message predominately with the use of essays and short stories.

I have a daily newsletter on armanitalks.com/newsletter where I share my message on soft skills with a global audience.

This is a just a brief introduction to me and I'm sure we will get to know each other more as the book progresses.

Introduction

Simplicity is the name of the game, my friend.

When the simplicity is focused on and repeated, the elegant complexity naturally presents itself.

Allow us to learn basic division so long division takes care of itself.

Allow us to **get to the point.**

Get To The Point

Part 1:
Fundamentals

What to Expect

Every essay writer should understand some basics that will make their journey much easier.

A few of the basics include:
- Understanding what logic is.
- How to be a critical thinker so we can solve problems better.
- Understand what words are.

'Understand what words are? Doesn't everyone know what words are?'
No.

Get To The Point

In this section, we will cover the fundamentals so you have **conviction** behind your words.

What is Logic?

Logic is a series of:
- Because of this, this happened.
- Because of this, this happened.
- And because of this, this happened.

The connections of 'because of this, this happened,' is the bedrock of all scientific studies.

The connections of 'because of this, this happened,' allows for backward and/or forward thinking.

Allow me to give you a pretty dark example.

Imagine that you walk into a room after hearing a woman scream.

You walk in and see that the woman has a black eye. Next to the woman is a man who has an empty alcohol bottle in his hand.

What are some conclusions you can make?

This is when we activate backwards thinking of:
- Because of this, this happened.

If I'm just spit balling, I would say:
- The man must have been drinking.
- Since he was drinking a lot, he must have gotten violent.
- Once he got violent, he let his fists fly.

This is a very simple idea of me going backwards to try and assess what happened.

All logic can instantaneously be warped with more information.

Fundamentals

Added information comes in saying that this woman is notorious for setting up people to ruin their lives.
Now my series of logic will be completely different!
- She saw that this man was drinking and wanted to frame him.
- Since he was drunk, he would not have the ability to clearly explain himself.

Having more information of the woman's past can tilt the
'because of this, this happened' to a new direction.

New information can always sway things.

Therefore, we should always be in learning mode, **especially** when we are using logic.

Someone who has little information in their database will often jump to conclusions.

Get To The Point

There is not much fluidity when they are hopping from point to point. Everything is abrupt.

They may say something along the lines of:

- A dog is an animal.
- So, all animals are dogs.

Huh??

This is an outlandish example but take a little bit of time to think of someone who lacks much logic. We all know a person like that.

They are impulsive, get brainwashed easily, make biased conclusions like they get paid for it, and routinely exercise poor judgment.

This is the type of person who is hopping all over the place.

The more essays you write, the more you will be forced into using logic.

Fundamentals

Just understand that logic comes down to a series of:
'Because of this, this happened' connections.

And for us to make the best logical conclusions possible, we must make sure we are accumulating as much relevant information as possible.

Fundamentals

What is Critical Thinking?

If logic is potential energy. Critical thinking is kinetic energy.

This is when we are bringing the logic to life by using the logic on real world scenarios.

One example is when you run out of toothpaste. All stores around you are closed at the moment.

You REALLY need to brush your teeth.

What do you do??

Get To The Point

This is the perfect time to leverage some logic to tap into critical thinking.

Critical thinking and experimentation go hand in hand.

Maybe you squeeze the toothpaste and it does not give enough paste.

This is a mild form of experimentation.

The level of desire will dictate how much experimentation goes on.

You REALLY need the toothpaste bud. Your breath smells like some stepped-on poop and didn't notice.

That's when the urgency leads to more experimentation.

Right now, you need pressure.
With pressure, the tube will get the residue of toothpaste to the top.
Enough for 1 squirt.

1 squirt is all you need until the stores open.

Rather than trying to squeeze the top of the tube, you begin from the bottom. Not only do you begin from the bottom, you get crafty with it.

This is when you are gently rolling the bottom tube into a circular motion adding additional pressure.

Toothpaste begins flowing out.

This leads to a fascinating discovery!

You not only have enough toothpaste for 1 squirt, but for at least 4 more squirts.

- Experimentation led to critical thinking.
- Critical thinking led to added pressure.
- Added pressure led to additional squirts.
- And the additional squirts saved another trip to the convenient store.

Get To The Point

If logic is:
- Because of this, this happened.

Critical thinking is:
- If I do this, this will happen.

Understanding Words

You understand logic.
You understand critical thinking skills.

Now is the time for words.

Did you know when reading was first becoming a thing, it was often known as 'guessing'?

'Huh? What do you mean? When I read words I know exactly what is being said.'
You THINK you know exactly what is being said.

Get To The Point

However, we will never **fully** know the intent of the author, the use of language during the times, and the context of the content.

One example is the word:
- Stink.

If I say:
Hey Jacob, you have a stink to you.

How do you think Jacob would feel?

'Jacob would be furious!'
Why do you say that?

'Because stink implies a bad meaning.'
Yes, to you.

But if you go back 200 years, saying someone had a stink to them was a compliment. It was equivalent to them saying:
Jacob, I really love your cologne.

By understanding that words are malleable, we should be extra mindful. A lot of times, words can be misinterpreted.

A great essayist should not get cute with it.
- Simple language beats complex language.

This is difficult to digest because we were often rewarded for getting cute with it as youngsters.

Where we were learning big words, using flowery language that did not move our point forward, and using words for the sake of meeting a word count.

All that may work in school, but in the real world, it's all about keeping it simple.

What else are words?
'Uh… symbols.'

Correct. What do these symbols represent?
'Uh… I don't know.'

Get To The Point

The symbols represent life.

Science is the study of space, time, and causation.

Words allow us to experience our surroundings and make meaning of it so our internal world can process the data.

Then the meaning we create in our subjective world can be relayed back to the external world.

Words are tools for essay writing.
Fall in love with words.

Supreme intelligence of words is known as linguistics intelligence.

Fundamentals

Get To The Point

Part 2:
What are Essays?

What to Expect

In the last section, we learned some of the fundamentals that ranged from logic, critical thinking, and words.

In this section, we are going to use the fundamentals to get a big picture view of essays.

If someone has never seen an elephant before...
- Would it be better to show them one body part of the elephant at a time?

Or

- Would it be better to show them the entire elephant first, so each body part makes more sense?

'The second one!'
Why?

'Because with the big picture view, the individual components have context.'
Correct.

Likewise, with a holistic understanding of what essays are, we are going to understand what the themes, styles of essay writing, and words all have to do with each other.

In this section, we will learn about the purpose of essays, popular styles of essays, difference between essays and short stories, and how to make a point.

Essay Writing 101

> *Essays are a collection of words intertwined to make a point.*

The point will depend on the type of writing style that you chose.

There are tons of essay writing styles that will depend upon the context, situation at hand, and the response you are trying to elicit.

Sometimes, an essay will be describing a certain situation step by step. The point is to recapture the situation in word format and transmit it to the reader's mind.

Get To The Point

Another type of essay is intended to expose the weakness of a point.

If you are someone who despises standardized tests, then the point of your essay would be to use logic to break down why standardized tests are not beneficial to students.

Another essay style is to inspire change. Let's say you don't only want to break down why standardized tests are useless, you also have a solution to replace the tests. The point of your essay is to break down your solution and get the reader envisioning the alternate path.

Getting to the point is dependent upon the type of essay that you are writing.

Popular Types of Essays

There are a lot of essay styles out there. Let's talk about a few of the most popular ones.

Arguing/Persuasive

Arguing is often annoying in conversations. But arguing is very good in the world of essay writing.

This is when you are exposing the weakness of a point to persuade the reader to take another path.

One example that I have with this style is when I break down the negative stigma of failing.

Growing up, I was not a big fan of formal education. I didn't like tests.

I had a problem where I would study a lot for the test...
But on the day of the exam, I would not do well.

So, there was a personal vendetta against tests!!

As I started ArmaniTalks, I realized how much I needed to fail in order to learn public speaking. Without failures, progress in public speaking would have been tremendously reduced.

My vendetta against the formal education system became reignited and I wrote an essay on the value of failing.

The essay used logic to share how failures were just as important as wins for the process of learning. Rather than labeling things as 'failures' so much, it would be wiser to view it as 'data.'

From there, I proposed an alternate solution to formal education. Rather than having so many tests in school, have more labs. Labs allow students to get their hands dirty and allow them to fail!
Failing in this context is another word for tinkering. Tinkering is the mother of true understanding. This is the type of understanding that a multiple-choice exam could never give.

This arguing/persuasive style of essay writing is often born from passion.

- What irks you?
- Or what do you love?

Don't allow the passion to make you unhinged and biased. Do your best to see the case of the other party as well. I get why formal education has tests. It's an easy measurement tool as a school system scales.

Get To The Point

Once acknowledging the pros of the other side, surgically use logic to tear the other side apart and propose your solution.

Critical Analysis

This style of essay writing is not arguing for anything or choosing any sides. Instead, it's just getting an idea and breaking it apart.

One example essay topic is:
Analyze the role social media will play on the culture 100 years from now.

This is when the essay writer will spend time accumulating knowledge on communications technology, social media's effects on different age groups, and the role technology and culture played on each other throughout history.

From there, the writer uses logic on a forward-thinking style.

Finally, they can propose their predictions.

This type of essay writing allows the essayist to develop a deeper understanding of the field.

Process/Explaining

The point of this essay style is to give directions.

An example is how to make eye contact with someone when you're nervous.

This essay may include the role of eye contact in communication.
Then the essayist will share a systematic process on how to look someone in the eyes, how to break eye contact, and how to have a gentle squint in the eyes.

This type of essay removes guesswork and allows the reader to follow a simple guide to go from:
- A->Z

A lot of restaurant owners are given pockets of essays describing how certain machines in the restaurant works.

Get To The Point

The owner is given the processes so they can run their systems without much trouble and have reference material for future employees.

These popular essay styles can often be intertwined with one another depending on the topic.

Difference Between Essays and Short Stories

Essays and short stories often get confused for one another, however, they are different.

-Essays lead with logic.
-Short stories lead with narrative.

Okay, with the difference out of the way, here's an idea:
- COMBINE THE 2.

Get To The Point

Combining essays and short stories into 1 is an intermediate to an advanced move. However, if you are capable of using logic **and** narrative, then the essay will have a profound impact on the reader.

An example is when the essayist is trying to:
- Explain why a cat is a better pet than a dog for a busy entrepreneur.

The essay can have a series of logical points breaking down:
- How cat food is cheaper than dog food.
- How cat's come potty trained where dogs have to be taught where to poop.
- Cats do not have to be taken for walks while dogs do.
- How the annual shots of a cat are cheaper than the shots for a dog.

A lot of facts, data, and graphics, great! You're making your point like a star.

But to make your point like a SUPERPSTAR, how cool would it be if you added a personal anecdote of when you had a dog and a cat?

Then you detail your first-hand experience with both animals?

Adding a story into an essay requires judgment.

If your goal is to be purely objective, then the story may do more harm than good.

But if you are writing on a personal blog, then the story will allow the reader to further understand your point.

This form of writing is also known as edutainment.
When the world of education and entertainment shake hands.

This is a very new look into essay writing that should have the essayist tingling with enthusiasm.

Get To The Point

'Are you saying I don't have to make my points in a dry and rigid way?'
Correct!!

Don't get so caught up in the process of the writing that you forget who you are writing to.

You are writing to a human.

The average human is bored a lot throughout the day. They live their life on repeat mode without even knowing.

If your essay can educate them, and dare I say, make them laugh…. then you begin separating yourself from the herd.

Making a Point

Making a point is dependent upon the essay that you are writing.

Average essayists start with the content and pray that the context will present itself.

Great essayists start with the context and see the content present itself.

The context can be difficult to grasp for a novice essay writer.

Get To The Point

Because it's easy to physically see the content which includes the words, the grammar, the punctuation and all that.

But the context is the **invisible** glue that holds the entire essay together.

It's the theme!!

'How can I teach my mind to think in themes?'
There are a variety of ways.

My favorite way is to simply ask:
- *What is the GIST of what I'm trying to say?*

Don't underestimate this question at all.

This question will spark the *chain* that gets the mind thinking in themes.

It's because you are getting a big picture understanding of the essay at hand.

The mind has signal and noise:
- Noise is the junk.

- Signal is the meaningful information.

When we ask:
'What is the GIST of what I'm trying to say?'

Slowly, a signal starts to emerge in the mind and the noise can easily be spotted + discarded.

The GIST method is just one way.

Popular author, R.L Stine, is one of the most prolific writers of all time. He is the creator of the Goosebumps and Fear Street series.

Do you know how he thinks of the context?
'How?'
He starts with the title first.

Just imagine!
This is a complete flip from what a lot of other authors do. A lot of authors finish their body of work, then create the title.

Get To The Point

However, R.L Stine uses the title to understand the context of the book.

From the context, he creates a skeleton (outline) of what the story will look like. Once he has the outline, he says:
'The story just writes itself.'

If you are struggling with the context, you can simply create the title first.

'My Thoughts on Racial Injustice in 2022.'

This title will allow you to reverse engineer your essay into existence.

Congrats! You're setting the stage to make some powerful points.

What are Essays

Get To The Point

Part 3:
Research and Development

What to Expect

It's hard to be cocky when you are in lifelong learning mode.

When you see a cocky person, assume their learning has ended.

An essayist who stops learning will immediately begin to doubt themselves. It'll feel very difficult to create. Writer's block will keep emerging left and right. Plus, the essayist will be heavily biased because they are ignorant.

Research is a key part of being an essayist.

Get To The Point

In this section, I'm going to share the traits of being a lifelong learner, how to learn from reputable sources, and how to use personal experience to gather meaningful information.

Let's begin.

Research and Development

Know
A Lot

The more you know, the more you can keep creating.

Therefore, it's essential to be a polymath in the making to be a prolific creator.

If you want a blueprint on lifelong learning, then be sure to check out my book, Modern Day Polymath.

Ray Kroc of McDonald's was able to globally grow his franchise.

Get To The Point

He knew it was not just about selling hamburgers. It was about making sure McDonald's standardized the process of making burgers.

What Ray thought of next was fascinating. **He created Hamburger University for all upcoming franchisees.**

These franchisees would learn the history of McDonald's, the processes, and how to spot quality ingredients.

McDonald's is arguably one of the most famous fast food companies out there. Despite their astronomical success, they stress the importance of research and development and are hungry to be in lifelong learning mode.

Get it... McDonald's......hungry...
crickets
Tough crowd!

To be a lifelong learner, you need to be hungry.

Research and Development

'Why do people stop being hungry when it comes to lifelong education?'

It's because they mistakenly apply physical laws to the mental world.

If I eat a bunch of food at a buffet, then I will be full. Once I am full, I will stop eating. This is the physical reality of the situation. My stomach can eat just so much food.

Subconsciously, a person applies the same mindset to their mental world. They are like:
'I can only consume so much, eventually, I am going to be full.'

The day they are "full", is the day their learning stops.
Instead, assume that you will learn **forever.**
Don't consume with 0 purpose. That's analysis paralysis in the making.

Consume with the intent of creating.
'Creating what?'

Get To The Point

Creating powerful essays that will outlast you!!

Be hungry.
Say:
'I will learn forever.'
Then, learn forever.

Research and Development

Reputable Sources

In this era, it's difficult to spot what is quality information and what is junk.

A lot of trial and error is required.
That's the bad news.

The good news is that there are so many ways to learn.
- There are books which you can get for 5 bucks.
- Audiobooks.
- Podcasts.
- YouTube videos.
- Interviews.
- Healthy debates.

And much more.

'Which source do you recommend I get started with?'
That's completely up to you.

My advice is to find something that you already feel comfortable with, then add onto that.

For me, I'm a reader and a watcher.
Normally, I will spend a long time reading a subject that I am interested in. Then I'll watch interviews & documentaries as well.

If you're a listener, then start off with listening. Educate yourself in the field and keep adding onto that.

Eventually, one reputable source will recommend another reputable source. This is called interleaving learning.

- Multitasking is bad when you are stopping a task mid-way and beginning another activity.

Research and Development

- Multitasking is good when you are holistically mastering many things that are pointed towards a unified goal.

Some of the best research will happen when you initially started off on a blog. Then there is a hyperlink on the blog for a phrase that you don't know the meaning to. So, you open the hyperlink in a new tab.

You continue reading the blog.
Then another hyperlink comes which you open in another tab.

Now you automatically have 2 new subjects that somehow intertwine with the initial topic that you planned to write an essay about.

These 2 new subjects may give you a completely different understanding of the subject at hand.

You never know which content piece can give you that aha moment.

Get To The Point

In one of the new tabs you opened, there may be a couple of book recommendations for other reputable sources.

Reputable sources can also be referred from teachers, peers in a mastermind, friends etc.

However, it's smart to develop your personal process for scoping out reputable sources.

The more content that you consume, the more you will develop a feel for quality material vs junk.

The main tip is to start off with the channels that you are the most comfortable with, and gradually add onto that.

Personal Experience

Some of your best essays will come from personal experience. These are first hand experiences that adds a dimension of relatability to your writing.

You have been through a lot of experiences:
- That's the data.

But how often do you introspect on the experiences that you have been through?

The beauty with essay writing is that it will bring you into eye contact with yourself.

Get To The Point

Introspection is a mighty technology to learn about yourself on a deeper level.

Say:
- I have a mind and body.

You will objectify yourself.
From there, just go where the feelings go.

Personal experience can be used in an essay to further add to your point. Don't get so carried away with your personal experiences that your essay starts losing its logic. Instead, be strategic when adding in anecdotes and such.

The more you introspect, the more you **mine your experiences.**

1. With a gold watch company, they mine the field.
2. Within the field, they extract gold.
3. When they have the gold, they put it through a manufacturing company that turns the gold into a gold watch.

Similarly:
1. An essayist mines their experiences (introspection).
2. Within their experiences, they extract wisdom.
3. When they have the wisdom, they put it through a manufacturing company (subject of the essay) that turns the wisdom into an essay.

Research and Development

Part 4:
Creating a Skeleton

What to Expect

Planning out your essay will make your life much easier. It's like you have a GPS and now you are just following directions.

- Some people like to be very detailed with their outline.
- Some people are very general with their outline so they can surprise themselves when writing their essay.

In this section, I'm going to talk about the importance of outlining your essay and how to do it for dummies.

I mean, for smart people.

Importance of Outlining your Essays

An outline gives you direction.
We bought up the signal and noise earlier.
- Signal is the meaningful information.
- Noise is the junk.

An outline allows you to spot the signal from the noise with **ease**.

Without any outline, everything will seem like a signal and you will risk rambling in the word format.

Get To The Point

Not only is the outline a great way to have direction, it's also a fun way to *ease* yourself into the writing process.

Picture creating an outline as adding training wheels to a bicycle.

Maybe one day, you will outgrow the outline. But do not be surprised if outlining just becomes a part of your writing process. Something you cannot live without.

With outlining, you will make essay writing an *assembling process.*
A lot of great companies do not keep building stuff from scratch. As they evolve, they consider themselves the assemblers of x, y and z.

When you have a strong outline, you build conviction behind every word of your essay. With conviction, imposter syndrome melts away. Without imposter syndrome, you can write with power, logic, and clarity.

Creating a Skeleton

So, the outline gives:
- Direction.
- Confidence.
- Turns essay writing into a process of assembling.
- And makes the writing journey fun.

Formal Outlining Method

The formal method is to get a neat piece of paper or Microsoft Word document.

From there, create the big why of your essay, bullets, and sub bullets.
'And?'
There is no 'and.'
That's it.

To give you an example...

Big Why (Gist) - *The purpose of this essay is to highlight why basketball is the best sport to play for busy professionals who struggle to maintain a social life.*

- Introduction – Give an overview of what to expect in the essay.
- Point 1 – Simplicity of basketball.
  - The rules can be learned in a day.
  - Few items are needed.
  - Does not require too many members to play.
- Point 2 – Cultivates a teamwork mindset.
  - Basketball teaches team work.
  - Teaches the players to participate in a system and work towards a unified goal.
- Point 3 - Great networking event.
  - Basketball allows for communication while in the game.
  - Friendship is a built when a group tackles challenges together.
- Point 4 – Personal anecdote to drive the point home.
  - Tell story of how I used basketball to grow my friend circle when I moved out of state.

Creating a Skeleton

- Conclusion – Highlight main points and give a call to action.

All I needed to create this outline were 3 variables:
- Big why
- Bullets
- Sub bullets

The Template is:

Big Why (Gist of the Essay) –
_____
_____

- Introduction – (Give preview of what to expect).
- Point 1
    o Subpoint 1
    o Subpoint 2
- Point 2
    o Subpoint 1
    o Subpoint 2
- Point 3
    o Subpoint 1
    o Subpoint 2

Get To The Point

- Conclusion – (Summarize main points and give possible call to action).

Numbers are arbitrary.

Creating a Skeleton

Informal Outlining Method

To be informal, get a napkin.
Crumple it up.
And create your outline on the crumpled napkin.

Same 3 variables are needed:
- Big why
- Bullets
- Sub bullets

'Okay Armani, why the hell am I creating an outline on a napkin? And why the hell am I crumpling up the poor napkin for?'

Get To The Point

To eliminate overthinking and invite in fun.

Here's what often happens with essay writing:

- People get very stiff.
- When someone is stiff, they overthink.

When we are using a napkin, we automatically invite a level of play into essay writing. Crumpling up the napkin further allows us to turn this into an informal activity.

> *We aren't writing essays because we have to, we are doing it to decompress after a busy day!*

In addition to that, the napkin is pretty small. This allows you to get to the point quicker.

You'll be FORCED into only creating the big points for your outline. When the big points are captured, the content will just flow out...

Creating a Skeleton

Get To The Point

Part 5:
How to Create

What to Expect

You have created an outline.
Hopefully, you are itching to write the content!

A great essayist never creates and edits at the same time.
- They create THEN edit.

This is the biggest cheat code out there. There are a lot of veteran essayists who have no clue that this simple cheat code exists!!

Let me repeat this point because it is highly important:

Get To The Point

- Never create and edit at the same time.
  - Do one THEN the other.

In this section, I'm going to share the creation mindset, how to create a rough draft, and why the timer is your best friend.

Let's begin!

Creation Mindset

The reason that people struggle with creating essays or creating content in general is because they create and edit at the same time. But the 2 have completely different strategies.

- Creation should be fast and done with fearlessness.
  - Act like you are the only person in the world.

- Editing is more deliberate and precise.
  - Act like the world will see your writing.

With the creation mindset, we don't care about punctuation, grammar, spelling and all of that. Our only goal is to get our ideas from:
- Mind -> reality.

I can't overemphasize how important it is to create without a care in the world.

If you spent time on your outline, then you of all people should be creating fast. This strategy allows you to BULLDOZE through any overthinking.

You do not have a creativity problem. You have a deadline problem, bud.

Never create and edit at the same time.
- That's like clicking the accelerator and the brake at the same time.
- That's like trying to lose weight and gain weight at the same time.
- That's like trying to invite toxic people into your life while trying to cut them off.

Nonsensical!
Got it?
'Yessir.'

Okay, now you understand the creation mindset. Let's understand the beauty of the rough draft.

Rough Draft

The rough draft is exactly that, it's rough.

It has a bunch of the big points of your essay & its logical flow.

But it looks like a mess.
Heck, it looks a bit disgusting.

The imposter syndrome mind is like:
'You are supposed to be essay writing. But you are writing this junk?'

This is where essay writing and electrical engineering become very similar.

Get To The Point

Have you ever tried taking apart some of the digital products in your living facility?

If you look inside, a lot of the guts of the circuit are ugly. Wires all over the place, capacitors sticking out, and glue marks on the boards.

It looks hideous!

But the electrical engineer understands the process of building a useful product.

They are creating the functional circuit, then they decorate the circuit with a plastic encasing and buttons that the user can experience.

Likewise, we are building the circuit of our essay with the rough draft.

Over time, we will polish up the spelling, punctuation, and word structure.

For now, use the rough draft to quickly get your ideas out there.

Over Write

Here's a little note:
It's better to have too much writing that you can chop away vs having little writing that you are desperately trying to add onto.

This paradigm further allows you to be **free** in the rough draft process.

Whenever you're in doubt during the rough draft section, say:
'I'll take care of my worries in the editing stage.'

Get To The Point

Write as much as you can in the rough draft section. If you did your research beforehand and know A LOT about the topic, then writing a lot should feel like light work.

Timer = Best Friend

The timer is your best friend when you are creating essays.

There is something about knowing the timer counting down that builds urgency. It forces you to stop overthinking and start creating.

Get an analog timer or use the timer from your phone.

'How much time should I set on the timer?'

Whatever you think it will take you to create a rough draft, divide it by 2 or 2.5.

Get To The Point

If you think it will take you 1 hour, then give yourself 30 minutes or 24 minutes.

You'll notice the urgency causes you to focus only on the BIG points.

> ***Rambling in an essay is a luxury that is faced by someone who gave themselves too much time.***

But when you shave away the time, you:
- *Eliminate writer's block.*
- *Reduce overthinking.*
- *Focus on the big points.*

Therefore, set the timer.

And write fast...

Your goal is to turn the skeleton of the outline into a body of work that shows signs of life.

How to Create

Get To The Point

Part 6:
How to Edit

What to Expect

People often confuse editing with proofreading. But the 2 are very different. We will be getting to proofreading in the next section.

In this section, I'm going to share the philosophy of editing.

You'll see exactly why I said to never create and edit at the same time.

In this section, you will learn what is editing, what to focus on, and how to make your writing sound conversational.

What is Editing?

Editing is process of cleaning up your writing so it is pleasant to consume.

Editing requires:
- Eliminating redundant sections.
- Possibly adding in a few new points.
- Getting rid of awkward speech patterns.
- Fixing the grammar and much more.

Picture yourself as a movie director with a ton of power. There was a lot of film that was shot during recording.

Get To The Point

Now you are watching it back. You're like:
- *Take this away.*
- *Put this here instead of here.*
- *Add music to this scene.*

All the editing is being done with the sole purpose of bringing the main point to life so it is pleasant to consume.

Don't edit aimlessly.
Edit with the intent of asking:
- Does this move my main point forward or not?

If not, delete it.

My Editing Process

Editing becomes a ritual for different essayists. They will all share their philosophy of how an essay should be edited.

Here is my editing process:
1. Fix the red lines.
2. Eliminate junk.
3. Mentally re-read the content back to see if it flows.

1 *Fix the red lines*

I often write my essays on Microsoft Word. During the rough draft, I focused only on the ideas. I didn't factor in spelling, grammar, punctuation etc.

Therefore, I have a **bunch** of red lines staring at me!

This is when I zoom out, and begin reading through the content and fixing up obvious spelling and grammar errors.

There are some words which are misspelled that Microsoft Word didn't pick up, so I'll spend some time correcting that.

I aim to do this entire cleaning up process pretty **fast**. My mind is primed to automatically be on the next word or sentence as I'm fixing up the current word or sentence.

My main intention is to glide through this stage.

This is what I call fixing the low hanging fruit. This is the first walk through of the editing process.

How to Edit

Once I go through the entire document, then I begin step 2.

2. Eliminate Junk

In the rough draft section, I **always** over write. Therefore, I rarely spend much time in the editing section adding in content. It does happen occasionally. But for the most part, I go in with the intention of elimination rather than addition in this stage.

With a lot of the spelling cleared up, I'm reading through the content and getting rid of any:
- *Unnecessary words.*
- *Repetitive points.*
- *Awkward phrasing.*
- *And sentences that don't move my main point forward.*

This is the section that I'm **ruthless** on.

I run a blog on the ArmaniTalks website where I routinely publish ~1000-word entries. In the creation stage, sometimes the words go up to the ~1200-word range.

Once I'm done eliminating, I bring it down to 1024 words. For books, I've trimmed 42,000 words to 36,000 words.

Hey, what can I say? I overwrite on the rough draft section for a reason. I know the editing section will take care of that.

3 Mentally re-read the content back

So, I've fixed up the spelling, grammar, and punctuation. I eliminated a lot of the junk.

Now for the moment of truth.
Read the content back.

This is when I zoom into my writing so I can see 1 page at a time, click the spinning scroll button on the mouse, point it downwards, and gently read through my hard work.

This step is quite therapeutic if you ask me!

I mentally read the content to see if it sounds like me.
I don't want a bunch of words talking to me.

I want ME talking to ME.

I am my ideal reader and the exact target that I write for. Therefore, it makes it easy on me to see:

- *Does this sound like me or no?*
- *Whoa, the points are being made in a very realistic way.*
- *It's like this essayist is having a 1 on 1 conversation with me!*

I'll keep reading the content back until all the kinks have been ironed out.

These are my 3 simple editing steps:
1. Fix the red lines.
2. Eliminate junk.
3. Mentally re-read the content back to see if it flows.

Part 7:
How to Proofread

What to Expect

In the last section, we talked about editing. In that section, you saw that editing was not just busy work. Editing is what brings your writing to life.

There is polishing, rearranging, eliminating, and reading back.

Proofreading is the final step before publication.

This is when it's wise to go through the content one last time and make sure that you got your spelling correct, paragraphs are broken appropriately to suit the message, and the formatting is on point.

Get To The Point

There are 2 ways to do proofreading.
Let's go through each method.

|1 - Do it Yourself

The good ole' DIY method.

Proofreading your own content may not seem like fun. Especially when it felt like you went through **EVERY** word and a reader notifies you of a misspelling.

This hurts the ego.

But I would argue that proofreading your own work builds character. It allows you to oversee the ENTIRE essay writing process.

From the process of the big picture stuff like outlining.
To the detailed stuff like creating/ editing.
And to the *micro* stuff like proofreading.

Get To The Point

You are putting your reps into essays and this allows you to build a stronger love for words.

Go through the document and clean up any spelling, grammar errors, and syntax errors.

The do it yourself method is one of the finest ways for an essayist to master their craft.

2 - Hire Someone to Proofread

There are a lot of sources out there where you can hire someone to proofread. Fiver, Upwork, Wordy etc.

If you have the funds, then you can automate this step.

Overtime, you'll form a relationship with the proofreader who knows your writing style.

The process of finding the right proofreader for you is out of scope for this book.
Just know that there are plenty of services out there for proofreading.

Part 8:
PUBLISH!

What to Expect

> **Publishing is the art of making others aware.**

There are a lot of essayists who are not really essayists. They are theorists.

Or I like to call them arm chair essayists.

'If I was writing the essay, then I would have said this, this, and this.'

'Oh, I'm an essayist. I never published my work, but I have a lot of material, trust me.'

Get To The Point

'I'll get around to publishing one of these days...'

These are the sayings of someone who cannot be taken seriously.

You need to publish your work to make improvements overtime.

Allow us to understand the power of publishing.

Importance of Publishing

Publishing for the first time may feel very difficult. Especially if you are a lowkey person who doesn't want to have other people poke holes at your ideas.

But the important thing to understand is that publishing your work will get easier with time.

Create a content creation schedule and follow it.

Do not allow yourself to have much of a say.

Get To The Point

In 2019, everyone was publishing daily newsletters. I thought that was overkill. I did one newsletter a week.

After I consistently published my work, I gradually grew my audience. Once I grew my audience, I decided that I wanted more practice. That's when I began doing daily newsletters.

One thing with publishing your work is that it holds you accountable.

At the time of writing this book, I've published for 1100+ days without a miss. That's a lot of writing!

And since I have all that content, I was able to create the 101 short stories, essays, and insights series which is up to a whopping 4 books right now!

Therefore, it's important to not only be serious about publishing your work. It's also about creating a content creation schedule that will take all the guesswork out of it.

Read Back your Old Content

In section 4 of research and development, I talked about the different ways of accumulating information.

We talked about reading, watching, and listening during content consumption. Then we talked about learning from personal experience.

Well, reading back your own content is a hybrid of consuming other people's content and your content.

Get To The Point

'What do you mean? How is reading back my work similar to consuming another person's content? I'm the one who wrote it!'

I know...But you'll see that your writing style now vs your old content has evolved/changed so much, that it feels like a different person wrote it.

By old content, I'm talking very old. Maybe your first ever writing.

I have a simple philosophy:

> ***If you are not cringing at your old writing, that means you are not writing enough.***

Some people do not want to read back their old writing because they physically cringe.

It's like when Facebook decides to show you your old posts and you think:
'I can't believe I used to talk like that.'

Well, get over it!

PUBLISH!

This is a part of getting to the point.

As you read back your old writing, sometimes, you will be amazed.
You'll be like:
'I can't believe my younger self knew that way back then. What a great way to make the point.'

Other times, you'll be reading the content and thinking:
'Hurry up and get to the point already. You're rambling way too much!!'

The insights that you get from reading your old content can be directly applied to your new essays.

This will lead to further research and development which allows you to polish up your game some more.

- Great athletes always watch their film back.
- Great essayists always read their essays back.

Part 9:
Creating an Empire with Essays

What to Expect

Here are 2 predictions for the future.
1. Short form content is going to see a rise in popularity.
2. People will no longer be loyal to people, rather universes.

Allow me to explain both positions.

With an abundance of content on the internet, we are ironically taking a flashback in time.

Back in the days, oral storytelling was king. This was before books, plays, and movies.

Get To The Point

These oral storytellers needed to know how to get to the point so they could convey meaningful information to the masses.

As time went by, we started to develop technology. Writing became a thing, the printing press became a thing, CGI became a thing.

From there, we were introduced to long form content.

Nothing is wrong with long form content. An essay can be written in long form.

However, an essayist can use a bunch of *micro* essays to build a body of work and share their philosophy with the world.

This is a great way to make a name for yourself.

People will be loyal to universes.

Another byproduct of a lot of content is that it expands possibilities. When different content pieces are combined, it leads to the emergence of a universe.

Think about Marvel.

Back in the days, people would say:
- I'm a Spiderman fan.
- I'm a Hulk fan.
- I'm a Thor fan.

Nowadays, Marvel is making a movie with all 3 of them at once!

People are more loyal to Marvel rather than the lone superheroes.

The beauty with essay writing is that it is highly dynamic. It allows you present your ideas from multiple angles.

How to Create a Universe Formula:
1. Create content
2. Connect content.

Keep creating, publishing, and refining. Soon, one essay will inspire the other and you will have a universe in no time.

Practice Makes Progress

Essay writing is a craft.

A renowned craftsman never says:
'I know everything about this field.'

Instead, they say:
'The more I learn, the more I realize I have more to learn.'

Which is a good problem to have.

- The writing will become more fluid overtime.
- Useless words will fall off quicker.

- And it will be much easier to get to the point.

It's important to create a practice routine that works for you.

Due to the nature of the ArmaniTalks business, I literally write every day. I write on a variety of platforms ranging from the ArmaniTalks blog, newsletter, and Twitter.

That's my practice routine.
Make it the goal to develop your own practice routine and stick to it.

Which brings me to my next point…

Solidify your Writing Process

This entire book can be boiled down to:
1. Write essays to make a point.
2. Research.
3. Create an outline.
4. Create the rough draft fast.
5. Edit in iterations.
6. Proofread.
7. Publish.

You can literally steal this formula and you will have infinite content material.

If there is any part of the process you want to tweak, then give yourself permission to do so.

Get To The Point

The more risks you take, the better!

And if it doesn't work, then at least you know what doesn't work.

Generational Ideas

There is a lot of talk nowadays about generational wealth.
Make an immense amount of wealth that you can pass down to future generations.

> **A remix to generational wealth is generational ideas.**

How cool would it be if you can pass down your body of work to future generations so they can make eye contact with your:
- Philosophy.
- Experiences.
- Teaching style.
- Logic.

And much more!

Since we live in the golden era of content creation, anyone can create content.

It's just a matter of having the desire, consistency, and processes.

Essay writing is an evergreen skill.

That means you only get better with time.

Final Words

There you have it!
The beginner's guide to essay writing.

This book was simple and to the point on purpose. When you fill your mind with too many strategies, then chances are you won't begin.

With essay writing, it's about having a few tools to get started and then starting.

Truly wise people begin before they are ready.

After reading this book, you may still have doubts.

Get To The Point

We always have doubts.

But waste no more time.
Time is money.
Begin writing essays.

Essay by essay will grow your empire. Soon, you will have others reaching out to you and saying:
'Thanks so much for publishing that! You helped me perceive life in a new way.'

If you enjoyed this book and want to further follow the ArmaniTalks brand, then be sure to check out armanitalks.com.

This website has a lot of my content ranging from blogs, podcasts, videos, books, and much more.

Plus, I run a daily newsletter that shares a daily essay on improving your communication skills. Sign up here:
- armanitalks.com/newsletter

PUBLISH!

Thanks again for purchasing the book!

PS:
Get to the point!

– ARMANITALKS 🎙️🔥

Get To The Point

Word Play

101 Short Stories, Essays, and Insights to Improve Communication Skills

---

Word Play is a collection of 101 short stories, essays, and insights to help you improve your communication skills. This book discusses a wide range of topics to build a deeper perception of human dynamics so you can communicate with clarity, power & warmth. In Word Play, you will learn:

- How to form allies and grow a network from the ground up.
- The art of consistency and how to stay disciplined.
- How to stop people-pleasing?
- Fundamental truths regarding the field of dark psychology.
- Social dynamics frameworks to deal with difficult personalities.
- Mindset laws to handle doubt, limiting beliefs, and fear.
- How to build a thick skin so you are more responsive rather than reactive.
- The art of storytelling to communicate your message with impact.

PUBLISH!

Street Smarts

101 Short Stories, Essays, and Insights to Improve Communication Skills

Street Smarts is a collection of 101 short stories, essays, and insights to improve soft skills. The world is constantly changing, the ability to adapt is more important than ever. It is time to ditch old modes of thinking for new mental models that allow us to thrive in a complex world. In Street Smarts you will learn:

- Public speaking strategies to dominate the stage.
- Content creation frameworks to build a powerful brand.
- Methods on how to deal with loneliness and feel whole.
- How to unleash an attractive personality and form long-lasting connections.
- Hacks to shatter analysis paralysis and take purposeful action.
- Emotional intelligence techniques to thrive under pressure.
- How to learn faster and more efficiently.

Get To The Point

Limit Breaker

101 Short Stories, Essays, and Insights to Improve Communication Skills

---

Limit Breaker is a collection of 101 short stories, essays, and insights to improve communication skills. In this book, you will gain the skill set of gargantuan thinking. The ability to think large allows you to become a high performer and deal better with people. Each story is geared to enhance your perception and break limiting beliefs. Soon, you will become a Limit Breaker, and shatter one goal at a time.

In Limit Breaker, You Will Learn:
- Energy management strategies to become fearless.
- The ability to come back stronger after a breakup.
- How to use digital tools to create leverage and amplify your presence.
- Frameworks to build influence among others.
- Methods to keep your ambition strong to achieve greatness.
- Tactics to enhance creativity and become prolific in your field.
- Hacks to make networking easier so others come to you.

PUBLISH!

Idea Machine

333 Writing Prompts to Skyrocket Your Creativity

The Idea Machine is a guided journal filled with 333 creative writing prompts from a variety of topics. Topics range from storytelling, to poetry, to fiction and nonfiction.

Benefits of added creative workouts include:

- Clearer thinker.
- Sharper communication skills.
- Better ideas.
- Enhanced content for brand.

The Idea Machine will allow you to improve your essay writing skills along with your ability to deliver a message in a concise way.

Take your mind to new heights and express yourself like never before.

Get To The Point

Tough Love

101 Short Stories, Essays, and Insights to Improve Communication Skills

Tough Love is a collection of 101 short stories, essays, and insights to improve communication skills. Knowledge which has the most practical value is not easy to learn. Because it challenges a lot of pre-existing paradigms. Therefore, Tough Love introduces the readers to knowledge that will lead to becoming a high valued member of society to create a long-lasting legacy.

In Tough Love, You Will learn:

- How to turn struggles into learning opportunities.
- The art of engineering rituals to become a top performer.
- Public speaking cheat codes to step up and deliver your ideas with conviction.
- Storytelling concepts to turn lifeless information into magic.
- How to overcome shyness & build a strong sense of humor.
- Social skills principles to be more charming & break the ice with strangers.
- How to with the subconscious mind to unlock the coveted abundance mindset.